The Black Ice Poetry
Volume 21
By
Mike Keane
Copyright © Mike Keane 2020
All Rights Reserved
Cover Design by Mike Keane

Contents

Contents

1

Wait

Wait; waiting for the moment,
Waiting for the secret to arrive,
Stark naked in all of its glory,
Warts grow in the lumps and bumps,
The frills hide in the layers of fat,
Blubber on blubber;
The gasping wait in a strange land,
A dog barks at the chirpy birds
Floating high in the shivering leaves,
Watching life fly by on the old man
Never to leave the strange land,
Trapped in the good days long gone,
The quivering lips drag on a sizzling
Cigarette wet in the melting saliva
Leaking through the corner of the
Wrinkled mouth too old to smile,
So young to die,
The wait is over;
Wait.

The Auld Hand

The auld hand;
The auld bones snap in a creaking
Grip on reality,
A slow handshake loose in the grip
Of old age,
The sore eyes watery in a staggered
Stare at the tainted mirror smiling
Into the wrinkled face of a lost soul,
The outstretched hands stuck to the
Flaking wall damp on the bones bulging
Through the papery skin creaking in
The pain of a hard life,
A shiver runs down the twisted spine
Of old age,
The sore eyes bleed to be free,
A sudden release in the creaking
Grip on reality;
The auld hand.

The Loincloth

The loincloth wrapped tight,
Loose around the virile motion
Of a twitching arousal slowly
Moving through the night within,
Without the luck of a kiss,
A sloppy kiss wet in the saliva of
A disdained rebuke on the rough
Tongue gone soft in the night;
The powerful man chiseled behind
The audacious loincloth bulging
In the amorous mind gone soft
In the head going through the
Virile motions of the night,
Hiding behind the loincloth in
The darkest night.

The Quiet One

Let rip;
The quiet one to snake out
In a bubble about to burst in a
Blast from the past,
The quiet one to escape the gaping
Flesh gagging for more,
More of the same;
The stench of the sly one,
Slippery in the wry smile of contempt
In the grinding of the teeth for
The quiet one.

The Bruised Hand

The bruised hand;
A slight squint in the eye of youth,
Raise the arm to feed the hand in
A gentle caress of the small ball
Grooved in a reserved culture;
A lash of the ash to whip on the
Green bones of a gullible child,
A jealous strike on the hand that
Shook the world,
The pain soaking in the numbness
Of the hand turning black and blue
To ease the trauma of imminent defeat
In the hand hanging in the cold air for
The high ball flying far away to spite
The bruised hand.

The Mind

The mind;
Grow tall and wise in the greyness
Of the vibrant mind spitting out,
A slight prick on the finger of a
Wasted youth lost in a timber desk;
Click the long fingers close to the
Deaf ear of the wax weeping wild
In the tortured mind fearless of
The distant voices leaking through
The dark emotions in a strange land
Where people label you in a sinister
Burst of laughter;
Away now to be a prisoner inside the
Walls of doom,
Kick yourself back to life on the slippery
Slope of a rugged existence,
Too old to fly, too young to die in the
Last gasp flight to the other side of
The mind.

The Fuzz

The fuzz;
All yellow in a mellow glow of thorns,
A slight prick on the dirty finger to a
Sudden flash of light in the slight of
A green handshake on the yellow
Flowers dangling on the prickly firs;
Suck hard on the bleeding finger
Dripping in the watered down blood
To feed the rattled madness of the
Bleeding hand in the yellow flowers
Of the firs humming in the buzz of
The busy bees of a lost desire growing
In the firs.

The Place

The place;
Wet in the dampness of the misty
Sky trapped in the soft day swooping
Low o'er the houses rubbing shoulders
On the side of a mountain steeped in
A lost history of the good folk long,
Long gone to the graveyard of the
Forest lost in the trees of the wood;
Blown away in the landslide of the vale
Deep in the flowing turmoil of the
Castrated life of a wandering peasant
Spitting against the howling wind of
Shame wrapped in a shivering coat
Soaked in the stench of a hard life;
A place that never did you wrong
In the echo of a torn landslide to fill
The place.

Balls

Balls;
Make a balls of it,
The wetness in the shaggy mist spits
In gaping spurts to dance a powerful
Romance full in the energy of life;
Coated in the strength of a mad bull,
Roaring in the stamping of tired feet,
The bleeding hoofs locked in the horns
Of the mad bull roaring in the head of
A crazy mind to spite the stab in the
Back of another waiting to take the eye
Out of your head and the bit out of
The starving mouth;
Roll in it until you make a ball out of it;
Balls.

The Birth Of Pain

Birth;
Hanging on for dear life on
The slide of a heartbreak
Crashing on to the rocks of
A crumbling cliff falling into
The sea of life still standing
Tall and proud in the painful
Birth lashed in the labour of
A growing love full in the strife
Of a mother willing to die for
A child to survive in the final
Push for life in the slap of the
Cry for a gasping breath in
The stretch of the long neck
Pulled out in the backroom
Full in the warmth of the open
Hearth fire gushed in the flames
Dancing around the mother giving
Birth in the shadow of pain.

The Cottage

The cottage growing out of stone,
Still standing bravely in the battlefield
Of stormy weather lashed to the
Dying slates for o'er a hundred years;
Proud in the fight with a stark reality
Of a back room birth full of pain,
The glowing hearth of the open fire
Burning brightly for mother and child
To struggle on and on and on in a
Cottage made of stone born to live
Gracefully.

12

The Ghost

The ghost of the old hag haggard
To the evil bone splashed in the
Wrinkles of a weathered skin,
Tainted in the badness of the flesh;
Lower the head in a mocking shame,
The laughing smile scarred in the face;
The long road without a turn almost
Coming to the end of its tether for
The old hag still spitting words of shame
On the righteous brave walking in the
Footsteps of the haunting lament wet
In the black shawl of the ghost hanging
On the stooped shoulders of the old hag.

The Ice Window

The ice window;
Scrape the early morning frost cold
On the window pane with jagged
Nails aching at the worn bone;
The sleeping child still warm in the
Nest resting on a broken bed of rusty
Springs creaking in the lullaby rock of
Sweet dreams in the mind of the child;
Break through the cracked eggshell to
Fly the nest into a far away sky in a
Bright blueness to warm the heart in
The vitality of a precious youth through
The flight of the spirit within, without
You in the quest for the wisdom locked
In the secret of life looking through
The ice window.

What

What;
What are you going to do when you
Get bigger?
What are you going to do when you
Get bolder?
What are you going to do when you
Get older?
What are you going to do when you
Get colder?
What are you going to do when you
Get meaner?
What are you going to do when you
Get sly?
What are you going to do when you
Get tears?
What are you going to do when you
Get broken?
What are you going to do when you
Get blind?
What are you going to do when you
Get locked away?
What are you going to do when you
Get kicked?
What are you going to do when you
Get small?
What are you going to do when you
Get death?
What.

15

Fingers

Fingers;
Let the music ferment in the fingers,
The aching finger tips slide o'er the
Smooth metal cut in the frets to cry
Out in a rift of blues,
A gentle melody ringing loudly in the
Runaway mind to behold in the palm
Of the sliding hand of the fingers,
The buzzing strings drifting in and
Out of tune to a strange melody
Lost in the fingers.

Spring

Spring;
The revolution of youth stripped to
The bone in a dark land,
The slaughter wrapped in the rags of
A golden youth buried in the sandstorm
Warm in the blood of crimes against the
Humanity nailed to the bleeding coffins
Buried in the desert sand;
The torture and the rape of the innocent
Scarred on the flesh of the oppressed in
A smile of shame on the brave people;
The dead will rise again on the last day
To fly with the angels in the glowing sky
Kissed by the Son of Man;
The Spring will never fade away in the
Face of humanity,
The thunderous sky roars in anger,
Fly the flag of hope to cleanse the sins
Of a desert under siege to starve in
The place of thy birth;
The children of paradise drink the wine
And eat the bread in the crimes against
Humanity.

Streak

Streak;
The lanky streak of misery,
Falling into a heap of waste
The barking dog left behind,
A wasted desire stained in the
Lanky streak of misery;
The cock of the broken leg wet
In the purge on the rough bark
Of the starved dog going slightly
Mad in the lanky streak of misery;
Slow down the talent laced in the
Cry of the precocious youth gagging
For a crack of the lashing whip,
Boldly swinging in the hand of
The lanky streak of misery living
In a wasted desire of shame;
Streak.

The Swirling Trees

The trees dance in the swirling
Sway of the wild wind blowing
In the darkest hour before the
The dawn of a new day;
The crispy leaves sleep o'er the
Strong roots leaking in the strength
Of a deceptive calm before the storm
Is stoked back into a howling fury,
The flying seed spinning round and
Round in the sowing of the wild oats
To release the seed of love from
The swirling trees.

A Constipated Mind

A constipated mind consumed by the
Importance of adulation in the man
Deaf to the echo of bigoted hypocrites,
Dancing to the beat of their own voice,
A constipated mind warped by the dark
Side of a blinded moon;
A crying child shackled to a school desk,
The moon blue for you in the colour of
The black ink stained on the tender
Fingers of the crazed mind labeled for
A certain failure by the stank teacher,
Crippled by a lame laziness in the yellow
Smile of the evil teeth rotten to the core
Of a mad in the head lunatic dying of
A constipated mind.

Hair

Hair;
The wet hair dripping to a tangled
Dryness on the rough fingers
Caressing the flaking scalp,
The itchy scalp wearing a white
Coat of dandruff;
Wash away the pain flowing in the
Waved dance of the breeze blowing
Through the muted pain of the hair.

Cold

Cold;
A piercing flush in the heart pushing
Wildly through the numbness,
A kiss on the leaking valve gurgling
In a warm embrace to the beat of
The echo pumping in the heart;
A shiver aches the spine in a jerking
Lament of yore,
A stumbled limp in a missed heartbeat,
Vanished in the spiritedly dance long
Lost to the good old days shrouded
In the misty fog of youth masquerading
In the cold flush of old age.

Wet Rain

Wet rain;
The belting drops knocking hard
On the window pane,
The drooling water awash in the
Dirt of a crumbled life,
Gasping on the stardust of the
Fallen star,
A white lightening flashing through
The night sky,
A lonely rumble fills the night;
A stray wolf howls at the full moon
Glowing brightly in the lashing rain,
The belting drops knocking hard
On the window pane;
A ray of hope shines in the blue
Eyes of the stray wolf still howling
At the glowing moon.

Born

Born;
Naked to the bone,
Slipping through the waterfall of
A painful birth,
Hand in hand with the mother of
Life sleeping in a bed of damp sweat
Drying in the pain of labour,
A shrieking cry shivering in the lips
Of life to tumble head o'er heels in
The birth of a boy in the child;
Born.

The Dark Eyes

The eyes;
The eyes of darkness lost in
The eyes of a thousand births
Crying out in the tears of the
Redeemed;
The deep wrinkles crease a
Jagged furrow in the dark bags
Bulging o'er the crying eyes,
The long wry stare pierce through
The eye of the beholder,
Blinking in a slow blindness trapped
In the pupil of the darkness;
The eyelids sleep for the last time in
The eyes crashing on the rocks of the
Stormy sea.

Rigmarole

Rigmarole;
Same old thing in the rise and fall of
The burning sun,
Day after day in night after night,
The dim light sleeps in the arms of
The dying sun rising in the east of
The west awake;
Blink the tired eyes in a tender rub of
The raw soreness lurking on the eyes,
The bleeding tears leak through the
Wrinkles of old age in the same auld
Rigmarole.

Gone In The Head

Gone in the head;
Half past dead,
A lone survivor worn out in a
Frayed trousers crisp in the
Stiffness of a board,
The hidden legs sprayed in a
Virgin whiteness,
Better than the dirty wool soaked
In the oil of the sheep,
Half past dead,
Gone in the head,
Hanging on to a frail sanity by
The skin of the broken teeth,
Yellow in the life of the long day
Waiting for a new dawn;
Kiss the truth in the deep tongue
Of a life laid bare,
Gone in the head.

Laid Bare

Laid bare;
Sleeping stark naked on the warm bed,
The tank full to the brim in the flow of
Words torn apart by a figment of the
Warped imagination laid bare in the
Lust for words buried deep in the
Naked truth of the mind laid bare
For the last time;
The crazy bear will tear you apart.

Topless

Topless;
The flesh of life growing wild
In the breasts living together
Side by side sharing in the milk
Of humanity slowly running dry,
Curdled in the deadly heat of a
Perished land sagging in the flesh
Of a broken time sharp in the pinch
Of the boney fingers on a decayed
Flesh ripe for the picking in a drooped
Forgiveness;
Topless in life,
Bottomless in death.

Until

Until;
Death do us part in the only vow
Worth taking from the words of
The divine truth fit for a King
Without a Queen;
The man without a woman,
The woman without a man,
Death do us part;
Until.

Waste

Waste;
A wasted waste slowly evaporates
In the misty mirage to dazzle the
Blind eyes of the land,
Full of rejection to the fake image
Hovering o'er the glorious youth
Tangled in a locked embrace with
The old age of a wasted time
Banished to the wilderness
Forever more;
Waste.

31

The Glass Jar

The glass jar;
Walk the lonely road you always walked,
Hand in hand with the beloved mother,
Roaming down the dusty track wet in
The watery mist of a soft day;
A soft day thank God,
Heading for the little shop o'er the hairy
Brow of a hill lost to the mountain,
Mother hand in hand with the happy
Child smacking the lips soon to be
Coated in a rich sugar resting on a
Dirty counter full of a sweet treat in
The glass jar,
The smiling child happy at last with the
Eyes bulging on the bulls eyes buried in
The rough hand of the old woman lost
In the chatter of the gossip women
Poking fun at the happy child;
Walk the lonely road home,
Skipping hand in hand with the beloved
Mother holding tight on
The glass jar.

Squander

Squander;
The gutter shines in the face of the
Squandering lout too big for his
Stolen boots,
A roughian thug asleep in the bed of
A lowlife,
A good for nothing coward staring into
The face of the gutter in a blissful
Ignorance,
A dealer in the making of a fake life;
Squander.

Hay

Hay;
A great man to fork hay floating
High in the corrugated shed,
A gulping dust to clear the throat,
A spit in the choking mist to dampen
The spirit of the best man trapped
High in the hay shed of dust;
The golden hay full in the life of
A hard winter glowing in the dust
Of a sizzling summer smiling in
The saving of the hay,
The after grass green in the envy
Of a great man to fork hay.

34

Hard Times

Hard times are cold as ice stuck
To the frosty window;
A cold face early in the morning
Of a breaking day lost in the watery
Sun slowly melting the ice on the
Window pane covered in the cracks
Of the hard times lurking in the
Shadow of the striking hammer
Spitting sparks of fire in the smile
Of the toothless man with the hardened
Gums bleeding in the toil of the
Hard times.

Ride

Ride;
Throw the cracking bones of the
Auld leg o'er the creaking bicycle
Rolling down the road of the beaten
Path steeped in the reminisce of a
Better time lost to the past;
Metal on metal falling apart at the
Rusty seams in the crunch of bones
Turning the rustic pedals,
A dog barks in the distance to the
Rhythm of the creaking bicycle
Rolling down the road of the beaten
Path choking in the gasping breath of
A rusty decline;
Ride.

The Wild Child

The wild child;
Slightly touched in the head,
A bulging numbness in the veins
Through the busted mind;
The laughing hyenas dressed in
The clothing of a sickness wrapped
In a jealous intent of a lame betrayal
On the run from a stark reality
Warped in the mind of the wild child;
Not the full shilling in the rattle of
The loose change buried deep in
The pocket of a rattled lament
Scratching on the dirty coins of
The wild child;
Slightly touched in the head of a
Bulging vein numb in the busted mind
Of a bloodied shame tainted on the
Yellow tongue of the wild child.

A Shady Man

A shady man;
Slapped in the face of the boney hand,
The loose flesh clinging to the sagging
Skin stuck to the bone wasting away
In a brittle demise of a hanging life;
Young at heart in the beauty of old age
Furrowed on the brow of the working
Plough shining in the light of
A shady man.

The Soaked Stumpery

The soaked stumpery;
All alone tangled in the middle of
A mystic wood growing wild in
The grove alive with poisonous
Mushrooms hiding in the moss
Wet in the early dew drops
Dripping from the towering trees
Sheltering the soaked stumpery
Slightly shivering in the rays of
The morning sun flickering a ray
Of light o'er the forest awash in
The nature of life running through
The spine of the soaked stumpery.

Propensity

Propensity;
Riddled in the name of the game
Trapped in the gaze of the player
Straddled in the saddle of fame;
Fabled in the glowing mane of the
Strutted beast taking the player
Away into the light of the starry
Night staring deep into the eye of
The blind beggar lost in the dark
Side of the troubled mind rooted
In a stale madness of a possessed
Propensity straying hopelessly into
The dark light of the fading night.

40

Plans

Plans;
Rarely work out when put into action,
The good ones stray away into the
Mind of a stumbling drunk dragging
Himself on the road to nowhere;
People make plans dead in the water,
Standing naked at the window of life,
Others stop and stare into a laughing
Smile of intent wandering wildly astray
In the stumbling drunk dragging
Himself on the road to nowhere,
Falling head o'er heels to kiss the best
Laid plans into the gutter.

Hate

Hate;
Slated in the savage eye of the beholder
Full in the pride of a narcissistic mind,
Move along the painted line paved in
The hate of a vengeful slaughter on the
Innocent brave enough to roll around in
The fabled sand of vanity washed in the
Burning rays of delirium;
The jealous hatred condemn the good
Man into a wall of derision,
Too late to stamp on the stiff brake in
The stonewall crash of hate.

42

You

You;
Give it just to take it away in the
Blink of the burning eye,
Hanging on to the wire digging
Into the palm of the hand
Wrapped around the little finger
Raw to the bleeding bone,
Lick the saliva in the smack of the
Dog's tongue to heal the flapping
Flesh in the throbbing pain of the
Bone bursting through the skin,
You;
The crying eyes dry in the heat of
The labeled child old and grey before
The sun sleeps;
You.

The Crispy Leaves

The crispy leaves;
Fallen on the hallowed ground,
The crispy sleep on the grave
Without a headstone,
A slab on the creaking bed of
A toiled soil full in the dust of
A past life under the cover of
The crispy leaves;
Crispy to the touch,
Warm on the heart,
Softly vanish into the clay.

44

Life

Life;
Laid bare to flake away in the
Craggy cracks long and narrow
Through the winding twist of
The rock once molten in the fire
Of a sudden eruption ready to
Create life in the craggy cracks;
A stray butterfly lands on the craggy
Face in the flap of the golden wing
Flicking a moist kiss on the skin
Now so gay and full in the bosom of
Life.

The Pretty Girl

The girl;
Almost too pretty to be true in
A glorious love for a man full of
Honey in the painted lady of his
Dreams in the girl to have it all
And lose it all in the blink of the
Weeping eye;
The power of honey in the love
For the girl too pretty to be true
In another love lost;
The girl.

The Wire

The wire;
A tangled mess in the long hair,
Knots wet in a cruel blackness,
The skin itchy on the flaking scalp,
A sharp stab of the sharp nail to
Dig deeper into the flesh raw in
A tangles mess of the dark hair
Covered in black knots cutting into
The wire.

The Lover's Eye

Lovers;
Love at first sight in a smiling
Glance o'er the cold shoulder
In a loving desire to satisfy;
Fade away into a gush of wind,
Hide behind the half door to
Stab a shiver down the twisted
Spine shaking like a leaf green
In the envy of lovers entwined
In the love me of the love me
Not puffing on the daisy flower
Of a love blown away in the wind;
The lover's eye.

Walk

Walk;
The old path worn away in a
Crippled sience in the echo
Of the footsteps dragging a
Track through the worn path;
A dirt path paved on the side
Of the mountain wet in the
Misty dew of the early morning
Soaking through the rays of the
Sun beating a smile on the worn
Path drifting into the old age of
The mountain drained of life in
The ruined cottage once full in
The echo of warm laughter in
The snow spitting time of year;
The girl linking hands in the shy
Smile of the boy lost to the mercy
Of the mountain In the long strides
Of the mighty walk worn away in
The footsteps of a glorious time paved
In the walk of walks.

The Firs

The firs;
A vibrant yellow in the kiss of
The mist stained in the charm
Of the purple heather licking
On the yellow petals until strained
In the darkness of the night to
Wash away the sins in the purple
Petals to light the night sky brighter
Than the watery glow of the morning
Sun on the firs burning brightly in a
Yellow glow;
The firs.

50

Begging

Begging in a beg of lament;
Sat on the cold slab crying
Out for any spare change
Loose in the rugged hand of
The soft fist;
Stand tall and proud to walk
The fabled streets with pride,
Glancing at the dark clouds
Swooping low to bounce you
Into the sea that'll never change
In the spare change of life;
Sat on the cold slab dreary
In the mist of poverty,
Begging for a better life dressed
In the rags of a wealthy smile.

White

White;
White on white,
White on black,
Black on black,
Black on white
In the sizzle of the skin glowing
Brightly in the glow on the dark
Side of the moon blinking
White on white,
White on black,
Black on black,
Black on white;
Live graciously with each other
In the glow of the moon.

Legs Away

Legs away;
The stale sweat lingers,
Lashed to the legs stuck
Together leaking in a cold
Sweat to push the legs apart,
Kicking high in the legs akimbo
Dressed to kill in the fishnet of life
In the cast of an amorous shadow on
The legs away.

Black Ice Poetry 21

The dansant in the dark side of the
Mind;
Waiting for the secret to arrive,
Stark naked in all of its glory,
The frills hide in the layers of fat,
The auld bones snap in a creaking
Snap on reality,
A slow handshake loose in the grip
On old age;
Grow tall and wise before the mind
Weeps in the dampness of a soft day,
Dance around the mother giving birth
In the shadow of pain asleep in the
Backroom of a stark reality;
The black shawl hanging on the
Stooped shoulders looking through
The window pane dripping in melting
Ice of the early morning sun;
Let the music ferment in the fingers
Of a rage in the beat of the blues,
The trees dance in the swirling sway
Of the wild wind blowing in the darkest
Hour before the dawn of a cold day;
The crispy leaves asleep on the grave
Covered in a blanket of moss,
The yellow teeth cringe in an evil smile,
The muted pain of the flowing hair
Blowing away in the wind of change;
The misty fog of youth laughing in

The face of old age on the rack,
A lone wolf howls at the full moon
Hanging in the crying sky of the
Birth in a boy lost to the child,
The bleeding tears dripping through
The furrow of the wrinkled skin;
Gone in the head of half past dead,
Hanging on to a frail sanity by the
Skin of the cut teeth;
Sleeping naked on a bed of nails
Caressing the bare skin in the flow
Of words leaking from the tired
Mind alive in the sound of insanity;
Topless in the life of a bottomless
Death fit for a raging bull,
A wasted waste evaporates into the
Dark light squinting in the blind eye;
Walk the lonely path you always walk,
Hand in hand with the beloved mother
Holding tight on the glass jar;
A roughian thug asleep in the bed of
A lowlife green in the envy of a great
Man on the run from a certain doom,
Time lost in the past of the wild child
Touched in the head of the full shilling,
Slapped in the face of the boney hand,
The nature of life alive in the soaked
Stumpery shining brightly in the light
Of the fading night;
Fall head o'er heels to kiss the best
Plans under the carpet,

Too late to stamp on the brake of life,
Crashing into the stonewall;
Crispy to the touch on the cold hand
Of the warm heart to lose it all in the
Blink of of a weeping eye covered in
The black knots cutting into the wire
Bloodied in the stain of evil;
Love at first sight in a glance o'er the
Cold shoulder of a crazed love,
The old path worn away in a crippled
Silence of the mist stained in the charm
Of the purple heather to wash away
The sins of temptation;
Sat on the cold slab dreary in the glow
Of a painful poverty.

Books By Mike Keane

The Ice Gender Trilogy

Lackabrack In Time

The Homeless Gentleman

Born On A Cobbled Street

Cafe Sex

Still Here

Bag Of Bones

Black Ice Poetry(Volume 1-20)